The Third Day

by
Joe Pileggi

Illustrated by
Ellis Noone
and
Josiah Tower

WHP
Wyatt House Publishing

Wyatt House Publishing
Mobile, Alabama

Wyatt House books may be ordered through booksellers or by contacting:

WYATT HOUSE PUBLISHING
399 Lakeview Dr. W.
Mobile, Alabama 36695
www.wyattpublishing.com
editor@wyattpublishing.com

Because of the dynamic nature of the Internet, any web address or links contained in this book may have changed since publication and may no longer be valid.

Cover and interior layout by: Mark Wyatt

ISBN 13: 978-1-954798-12-0

Printed in the United States of America

Dedicated
to the One Who made
the third day worth celebrating

Aren opened his eyes. The stars were still shining but he couldn't sleep. He was too excited. Today was the day! Grandpa Ram said Good Shepherd would be coming here. He couldn't wait to see Good Shepherd again.

"Grandpa Ram, Grandpa Ram, wake up!" Aren said.
"Wha-a-a-t?" Grandpa Ram asked, still half asleep.
"It's today, Grandpa Ram, it's today! Good Shepherd
is coming today! You said so!"
"Yes, but it's still early…"

"C'mon, Grandpa, let's go," Aren said as he
began to trot down the road.
"Ok, OK, I'm coming. Wait up! I'm not as
young as I used to be," Grandpa Ram said as
he slowly walked beside Aren.

The sun was coming up and they could hear the noise of the people shouting. Aren could see them waving palm branches in the air.

"What are they doing?" asked Aren.

"They are welcoming Good Shepherd," Grandpa Ram said with a smile.

"He's here? I want to see Him." And with that, Aren ran ahead and pushed through the crowd.

As Aren looked up the road, he saw Him. Good Shepherd was coming toward him…and he was riding a donkey!

Good Shepherd smiled at everyone as He passed by and they called Him King. He came closer and closer to Aren. Then He was right in front of Aren and smiled.

Aren's heart beat fast and tears filled his eyes. "He remembers me… and He still loves me!"Aren ran to find Grandpa Ram. "He looked at me, Grandpa Ram! He smiled at me! He remembered me!"

Grandpa Ram said, "Yes, He does, Aren. Do you remember what He said to you when He brought you back to me after you ran away?"

"Yes." He said. "'I will always love you.'"

"That's right. And He still does."

Tears mixed with Aren's smile as he thought, "Yes, He still does. And He always will."

A couple of days after Aren had seen Good Shepherd again, Grandpa Ram told Aren, "Let's go for a walk."

"Where are we going, Grandpa Ram?" Aren asked

"To the Garden. I want to show you something," he answered.

Aren loved going to the Garden. It was so beautiful and peaceful. But it was already getting dark outside. Why are we going now, Aren wondered.

By the time they got to the Garden, it was almost dark. Grandpa Ram led the way until they came to a grove of trees. He stopped.

"Look over there, at that big rock. What do you see?"

Aren looked hard. "It looks like a man kneeling at the rock. Who is it, Grandpa Ram?"

"Let's move a little closer. I think you might know Who He is."

"Grandpa Ram", Aren whispered. "It's Good Shepherd! What is He doing?"

"He's praying for us, because He loves us so much." Grandpa Ram answered. Aren thought he saw a tear in Grandpa Ram's eye.

All of a sudden, loud noises of angry people filled the air. They were holding sticks with fire on one end and were walking toward Good Shepherd.

They made a circle around Him, grabbed his arms and led Him away.

"What are they doing to Good Shepherd? Where are they taking Him? We have to go help Him!" Aren cried and began to run toward Good Shepherd.

"No, Aren, wait! We cannot help Him now," Grandpa Ram said.

"Why not? He helped me when I was bad and ran away. Now He needs our help." Aren was crying and could hardly speak.

"Aren, look at me." Grandpa Ram said, as he reached down and lifted Aren's chin so he could look into Aren's eyes.

"One day when you were playing with the other lambs, Good Shepherd told the rest of us that bad things were going to happen to Him. He said that was why He came here as a baby. And because of that, we could not be with Good Shepherd forever unless Good Shepherd's Father would forgive us for all the bad things we have done. And there is only one way that His Father would do that."

"What way is that, Grandpa Ram?" Aren asked.

"A lamb has to die every year," Grandpa Ram said softly.

"A lamb? That's me! Do I have to die?" Aren's eyes were wide with fear.

"It could have been, Aren. And it could have been me when I was a lamb. But Good Shepherd said He came to change that. He said He was going to be the Lamb to die for everyone, forever. He even called Himself the 'Lamb of God.'"

"Wow! Good Shepherd said he was a Lamb?"

"Yes, Aren. That's why He has to die – for us."

"But He has not done any bad things. It's not fair," Aren argued as the tears started again.

"I know, Aren," Grandpa Ram said sadly. "But it must be for now. But there is good news, too."

"Good news?" asked Aren. "How can there be any good news? You just told me Good Shepherd is going to die."

"Because after telling us all of this, He said He would not be dead forever."

"What? What do you mean?" Aren was really confused now.

"Good Shepherd told us that on the third day after He died, He would come back to life!"

Aren couldn't speak. He just stared at Grandpa Ram.

"Yes, Aren, it's true. That's what He told us. Has He ever told us anything that was not true?"

"No, He hasn't…. ever," Aren answered.

"OK, let's try to get some sleep. Maybe we will get to see Good Shepherd again tomorrow."

Aren could not sleep, no matter how hard he tried. All he could think of was the time he ran away and Good Shepherd came and saved him from the lion and brought him back. Now He was going to die? It's not fair. "I should be the one to die," he thought as he drifted off to sleep.

Noise woke Aren and Grandpa Ram. People noise.

"Let's go see what's happening," said Grandpa Ram.

Aren jumped up and ran ahead
toward the noise. Everyone was
on top of a hill, so he had to
push his way through the crowd
to see what was happening.
What he saw took his breath
away. It was Good Shepherd!
He was on a cross. There were
nails in His hands and feet and
a crown made of sharp thorns
was on his head.

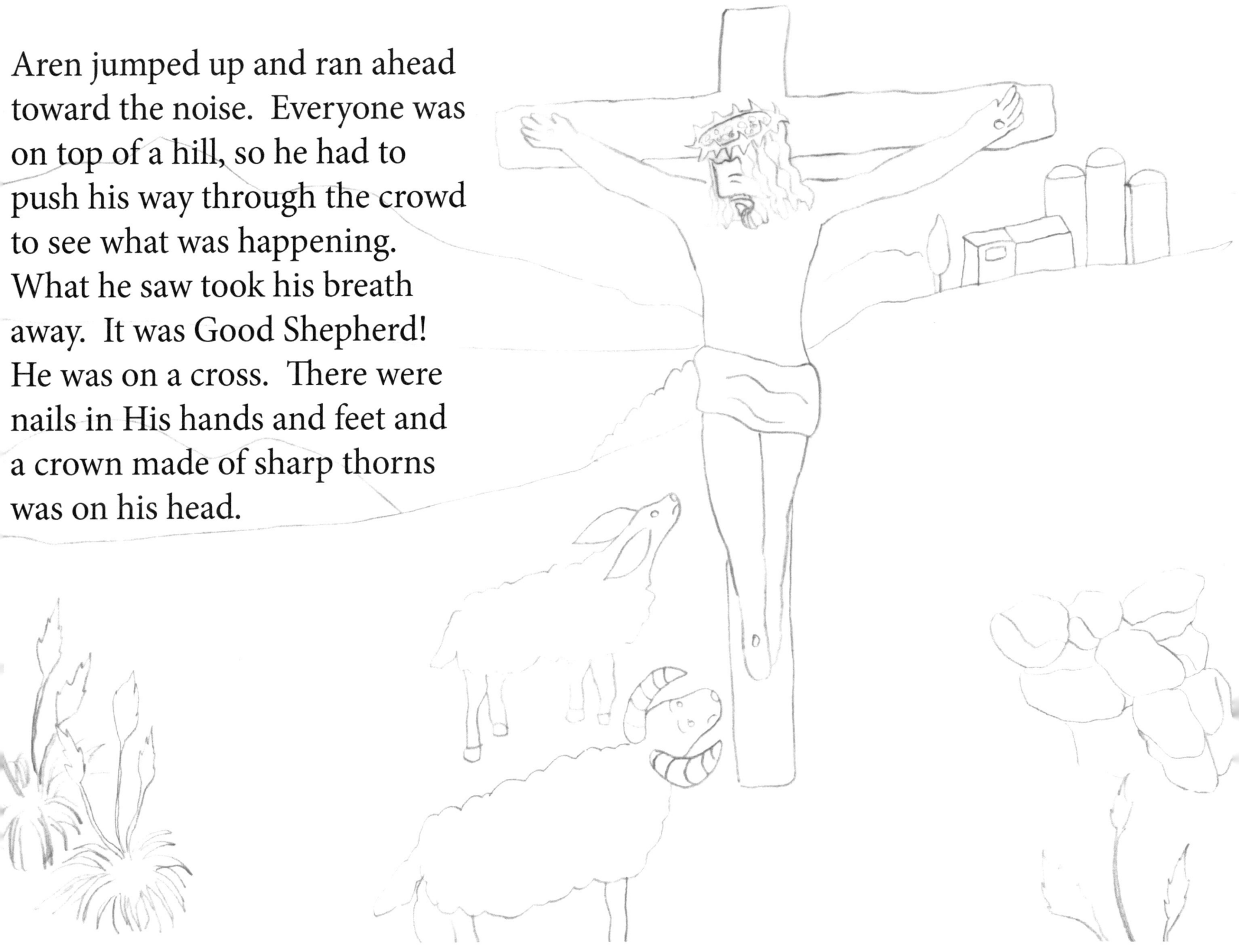

Grandpa Ram then came alongside Aren.

"Make them take Him down and take those nails out!" Aren screamed. "Make them stop!"

"It must be for now," Grandpa Ram said sadly. "But a better day is coming – soon."

Just then, Aren heard Good Shepherd's voice, the voice he had grown to love so much:

"Father, forgive them. They don't know what they are doing."

Aren looked at Grandpa Ram. "Forgive them?" he asked, with tears streaming down his face.

"Yes," Grandpa Ram answered. "Forgive. That's what this is all about. Forgiving us for all the bad things we have done."

Aren heard Good Shepherd's voice again: "It is finished."

It seemed that Good Shepherd looked right at Aren when He said it. Then, Good Shepherd bowed His head and died. Aren looked at Grandpa Ram. "Yes, Aren. It is finished. Let's go."

Aren couldn't stop crying. Good Shepherd was gone, forever --- no, wait. Grandpa Ram had said something about the third day. Could it be? Was there still hope?

Aren and Grandpa Ram followed the people who took Good Shepherd down from the cross and took Him to the Garden.

There was a tomb there with a big stone next to it. His friends wrapped Him in white cloths and laid Him in the tomb, then rolled the big stone in front of it. They cried as they left the tomb.

When they were gone, Aren ran and stood in front of the stone and called out, "Good Shepherd! Please wake up! It's Aren. I don't want you to be dead. Please come back to life!"   He couldn't say anything more. He was crying so hard.

"The third day, my son. We must wait until the third day."

Aren looked up at Grandpa Ram through his tears and said, "Then I will wait. Right here!" Aren walked over to the stone and laid down in front of it.

And there he waited, night – and day – and night – and day – and night. He would not leave to eat or drink. He tried to stay awake, but fell asleep on the second night until…. the morning of… the third day!

Blinding light chased sleep from his eyes and Aren woke up so suddenly it took him a minute to remember where he was. The Garden --- the tomb --- the stone --- Good Shepherd!   He jumped up and turned to look at the stone. It wasn't there! It was rolled off to the side of the tomb. Aren could see inside the tomb where the bright light was coming from.

But Good Shepherd wasn't in there. Where was He? Aren turned to look for Him but instead saw a man in a shiny white robe and a big smile.
"Are you looking for Good Shepherd? He is not here. He has risen from the dead and is alive, just like He promised!"
"Can you tell me where He is?" Aren was so excited he could hardly form the words. The man pointed toward the garden. Aren turned…
And – there He was!!!

Good Shepherd squatted down and opened His arms toward Aren. Aren took off running as fast as he could – right into Good Shepherd's arms. Good Shepherd scooped him up and brought Aren to His chest and squeezed him real hard. Aren looked into Good Shepherd's face, and saw the same smile and felt the same arms that held him the day Good Shepherd brought him back home.

"I told you I would never leave you." Good Shepherd said.

"But I saw you die, and I thought…" the tears started again.

"Yes, but now you see I am alive. I will never die again. And because you want to be with Me forever, I have forgiven all the bad things you have done, so don't remember them anymore, Ok?"

"OK," Aren said through his now happy tears.

"Yes, yes, anything…I will do anything for you, Good Shepherd," Aren said all excited.

"I want you to go and tell all your friends, everyone, that what I did was for them too. I want everyone to be with me forever – just like you!"

"O.K. I'll do it. I promise," Aren said.

"Good," said Good Shepherd. Now I am going to go to My other friends and then I am going to go to My Father. But I will come back to get you and your friends so we all can be together forever."

Good Shepherd gently set Aren down on the ground and gave him a kiss on the forehead.

Good Shepherd then lifted off the ground into the sky. "I will see you again…real soon! And remember, I will always love you".

"Do you think He will really come back soon to get us?" Aren said, still looking up into the sky.
"If you should ever doubt His promise, Aren," Grandpa Ram said. "Remember His last promise."
What was that, Grandpa Ram?" Aren asked.
The Third Day. Remember His promise about the third day."

Their eyes met. They both smiled. "Yes," Aren said. "He kept His promise on the third day!"

Author

Mr. Joe Pileggi was raised on a dairy farm in New York State. He grew up loving animals, and still does. He lives with his wife, Lori, and has 3 grown children and 6 grandchildren.

Illustrators

Ellis Noone is a native of San Jose, California and a graduate of San Jose State University. She now lives in Daphne, Alabama. She enjoys painting, drawing, crocheting, knitting, and designing and planting colorful gardens.

Josiah Tower is a native of Mobile, Alabama. Creativity has always been a passion of his life. He has a vision and goal to use his artistic gift to inspire the world about the wonderful God he serves, Jesus Christ. He enjoys drawing, illustrating, logo designing, music, and travel.

Wyatt House Publishing

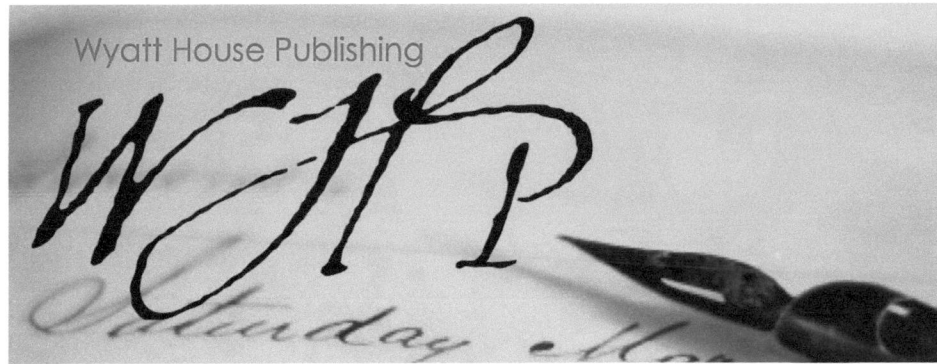

You have a story.
We want to publish it.

Everyone has as a story to tell. It might be about something you know how to do, or what has happened in your life, or it may be a thrilling, or romantic, or intriguing, or heartwarming, or suspenseful story, starring a cast of characters that have been swimming around in your imagination.

And at Wyatt House Publishing, we can get your story onto the pages of a book just like the one you are holding in your hand. With professional interior design and a custom, professionally designed cover built just for you from the start, you can finally see your dream of being an author become reality. Then, you will see your book listed with retailers all over the world as people are able to buy your book from wherever they are and have it delivered to their home or their e-reader.

So what are you waiting for? This is your time.

visit us at
www.wyattpublishing.com

for details on how to get started becoming a
published author right away.